SOUTHWEST WISCONSIN LIBRARY SYSTEM

3 9896 01491 9423

Dodgeville Public Library
189 Siowa Street
Dodgeville WI 53533

WITHDRAWN

D1712554

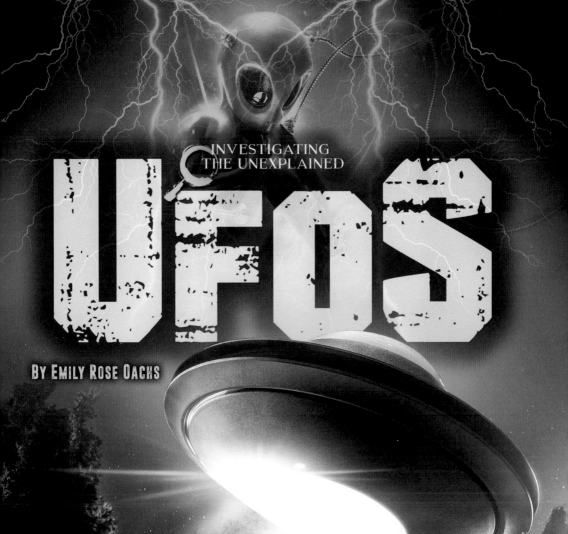

INVESTIGATING
THE UNEXPLAINED

UFOS

By Emily Rose Oachs

BELLWETHER MEDIA • MINNEAPOLIS, MN

BLASTOFF!
DISCOVERY

Blastoff! Discovery launches a new mission: reading to learn. Filled with facts and features, each book offers you an exciting new world to explore!

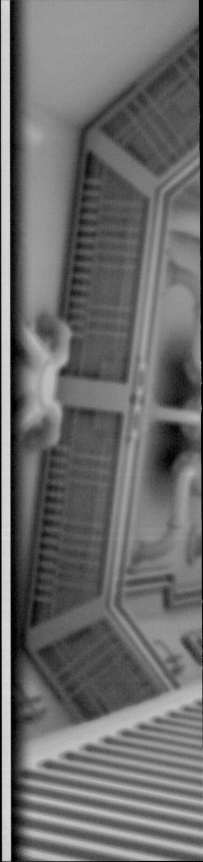

This edition first published in 2019 by Bellwether Media, Inc.

No part of this publication may be reproduced in whole or in part without written permission of the publisher.
For information regarding permission, write to
Bellwether Media, Inc., Attention: Permissions Department,
6012 Blue Circle Drive, Minnetonka, MN 55343.

Library of Congress Cataloging-in-Publication Data

Names: Oachs, Emily Rose, author.
Title: UFOs / by Emily Rose Oachs.
Description: Minneapolis, MN : Bellwether Media, Inc., 2019.
   Series: Blastoff! Discovery : Investigating the Unexplained |
   Includes index. | Includes bibliographical references and
   index. | Audience: Ages 7-13. | Audience: Grades 3 to 8.
Identifiers: LCCN 2018003592 (print) | LCCN 2018007111
   (ebook) | ISBN 9781626178564 (hardcover : alk. paper) |
   ISBN 9781681035970 (ebook)
Subjects: LCSH: Unidentified flying objects–Juvenile literature.
Classification: LCC TL789.2 (ebook) | LCC TL789.2 .O23 2019
   (print) | DDC 001.942–dc23

LC record available at https://lccn.loc.gov/2018003592

Text copyright © 2019 by Bellwether Media, Inc. BLASTOFF!
DISCOVERY and associated logos are trademarks
and/or registered trademarks of Bellwether Media, Inc.
SCHOLASTIC, CHILDREN'S PRESS, and associated logos are
trademarks and/or registered trademarks of Scholastic Inc.,
557 Broadway, New York, NY 10012.

Editor: Paige Polinsky   Designer: Andrea Schneider

Printed in the United States of America, North Mankato, MN.

TABLE OF CONTENTS

LOOK UP!

The night is pitch black. Marcus and Leila turn their car onto a dirt road. The road leads to a dark field. Unidentified flying objects, or UFOs, have been seen there. Marcus and Leila park the car. The UFO hunters rest on some large boulders.

Marcus nods off while they wait. Suddenly, there is a bright flash. "Marcus!" Leila shakes him awake and points. A glowing object hovers high above the clearing. Leila reaches for the telescope. Marcus stares at the sky in shock.

telescope

REC

5

The quiet, disk-shaped object slowly drops to the ground. It pauses for a moment before speeding back into the air. Smoke rises from the grass it touched. The object hovers for a few more seconds. Then it darts off in a flash.

The UFO hunters watch it pass over their heads.
It disappears in the distance. Neither Marcus nor
Leila can look away from the sky. They can hardly
believe their eyes. Was that UFO an alien spacecraft?

FLYING MYSTERIES

Strange objects are seen in skies around the world. Researchers find that almost all of these sightings can be explained after investigation. Yet some sightings remain a mystery. These are UFOs. Some people claim these objects are extraterrestrial spacecraft.

UFOs are nicknamed "flying saucers." Yet they take many different shapes, such as diamonds or triangles. Many simply look like strange, bright lights. UFOs also move in different ways. Some float above the ground, while others race through the sky at extreme speeds.

REC

triangle UFO

COMMON UFO SHAPES

light

circle

triangle

oval

disk

fireball

STRANGE SIGHTINGS

Mysterious **aerial** objects have been reported throughout history. Major modern sightings began in 1947. Pilot Kenneth Arnold saw nine UFOs while flying through Washington's Cascade Mountains. He believed they were traveling at more than 1,600 miles (2,575 kilometers) per hour!

That July, rancher William Brazel reported strange **wreckage** on his land near Roswell, New Mexico. He believed it came from a flying saucer. The United States government denied this. But the Roswell wreckage sparked much interest in UFOs. There were more than 300 reported sightings that year.

Roswell wreckage

Kenneth Arnold

EARLY ENCOUNTER

A 1639 account described a bright light darting across the sky. The light traveled back and forth above Boston for hours. It may be America's first reported UFO sighting!

UFO sighting
in Oregon, 1950

Staff of Project Blue Book

The U.S. government worried that UFOs might be enemy aircraft. They could threaten the country's safety. But they might also contain useful technology. In 1948, the Air Force launched investigations. Project Blue Book was the longest. It began in 1952.

The project's top scientists studied more than 12,000 sightings. They found explanations for most. In 1968, a government report argued the investigations were pointless. UFOs were not a threat. So the government ended all UFO research in 1969.

AN AREA FOR ALIENS

Mystery surrounds Nevada's secretive military site Area 51. In 1989, government scientist Bob Lazar claimed he studied alien spacecraft stored there. Many people question the truth of his claims.

SKY SEARCHERS

In 2015, the president of CUFOS helped start a project called UFODATA. Its mission was to build a network of machines. This system would constantly scan the skies for possible UFO activity!

Dr. Hynek (left)

Project Blue Book left hundreds of **credible** sightings unidentified. Former project investigator Dr. J. Allen Hynek believed some might be alien encounters. In 1973, he started the Center for UFO Studies (CUFOS) to pick up where Project Blue Book left off. CUFOS helps **ufologists** log and compare sightings.

The government was not finished with UFOs, either. In 2007, the Defense Department secretly reopened investigations. Researchers tested materials gathered from UFOs. They also questioned UFO witnesses. The program ended in 2012. But it was kept secret until 2017.

RB-47 jet

THE RB-47 UFO ENCOUNTER

In 1957, crewmembers on an Air Force jet had a puzzling encounter. Odd signals appeared on their **radar**. A powerful light then sped toward them! It darted around and trailed them through the sky. Radar on the ground also tracked the UFO. It disappeared and reappeared twice before finally vanishing.

Investigators studied the jet's radar signals and flight path. They also questioned the crew. The **evidence** matched up. Many experts have examined the case since. Project Blue Book determined the UFO was an airplane. Other investigators disagree.

THE RB-47 UFO ENCOUNTER PATH

Gulf of Mexico

1. **Gulfport, Mississippi:** UFO appears on jet radar
2. **Fort Worth, Texas:** UFO sighted on ground radar
3. **Mineral Wells, Texas:** Crew members see a bright, moving light
4. **Oklahoma City, Oklahoma:** UFO vanishes for good
5. **Topeka, Kansas:** Jet lands at Forbes Air Force Base

SCANNING THE SKIES

Ufologists use certain tools to search the skies. In most cases, UFO sightings happen at night. **Night-vision goggles** help spot objects in the dark. Telescopes let investigators study these objects more closely. If a UFO glows, a telescope can study it with a photometer. This device examines light.

Ufologists use computers to study UFO **databases**. Some databases log and map recent sightings. These help investigators choose where to go. Other databases track known aerial objects. Ufologists can compare these objects to the UFO they saw.

HOW PHOTOMETERS WORK

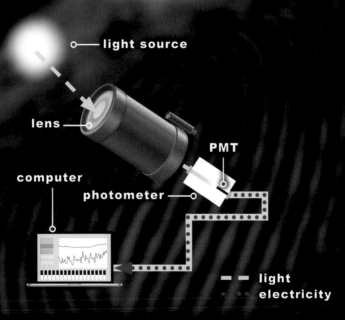

light source

lens

PMT

computer

photometer

- - - light
· · · · electricity

---

1. Light from a moving object enters the telescope lens.
2. Mirrors inside the telescope send the light to the photometer.
3. A sensor called a photomultiplier tube (PMT) turns the light into electricity.
4. A computer measures the electricity. This helps it track the object's speed and direction.

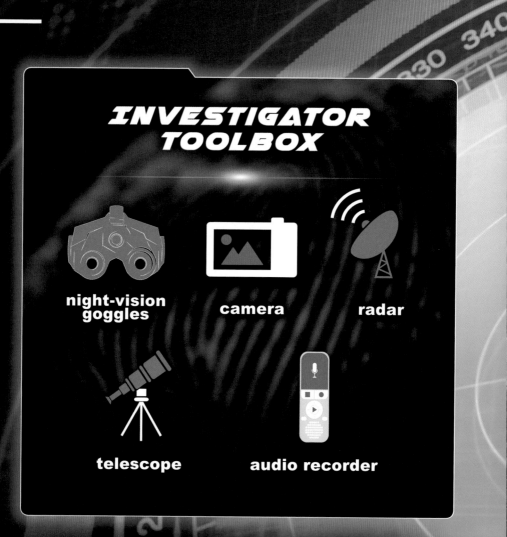

INVESTIGATOR TOOLBOX

night-vision goggles

camera

radar

telescope

audio recorder

Cameras allow investigators to record sightings. They can also document evidence left behind after possible UFO landings. Investigators share their photos and videos with other ufologists. They hope sharing information will uncover important UFO patterns.

350 360

THE TROUBLE WITH RADAR

Even ufologists admit that radar is not always trustworthy. Radar might show an object when none is there. Other times, it does not pick up on flying objects that are there!

radar

Radar devices also help investigators track UFOs. An **antenna** releases radio waves into the air. Those waves travel until they strike an object. Then they bounce back to the antenna. The device uses this information to create a picture of the object. It can show the speed and location of an aerial object!

audio recorder

Possible UFO landings may leave behind **physical** evidence. Investigators can then run tests on the landing spot and surrounding area. However, physical evidence is very uncommon.

UFO witnesses in Michigan, 1966

Stories from witnesses are key to investigations. **Audio recorders** are important for capturing every detail of these accounts. Investigators must question witnesses carefully. They need to separate the real encounters from the fakes. More witnesses usually mean a stronger, more credible sighting. Sometimes, investigators use **polygraphs** to test witness stories.

"MISIDENTIFIED" FLYING OBJECTS

In the United States alone, there have been more than 100,000 reported UFO sightings. Yet **skeptics** claim that most are easy to explain. They argue that many witnesses simply misidentified what they were seeing.

Some sightings are caused by space objects. Witnesses confuse bright planets, meteors, or stars for UFOs. Other sightings are actually weather **phenomena**, such as ball lightning. This globe-shaped lightning can float or move in strange ways. Witnesses also mistake human-made flying objects, such as airplanes or weather balloons, for UFOs.

meteor

ball lightning

weather balloon

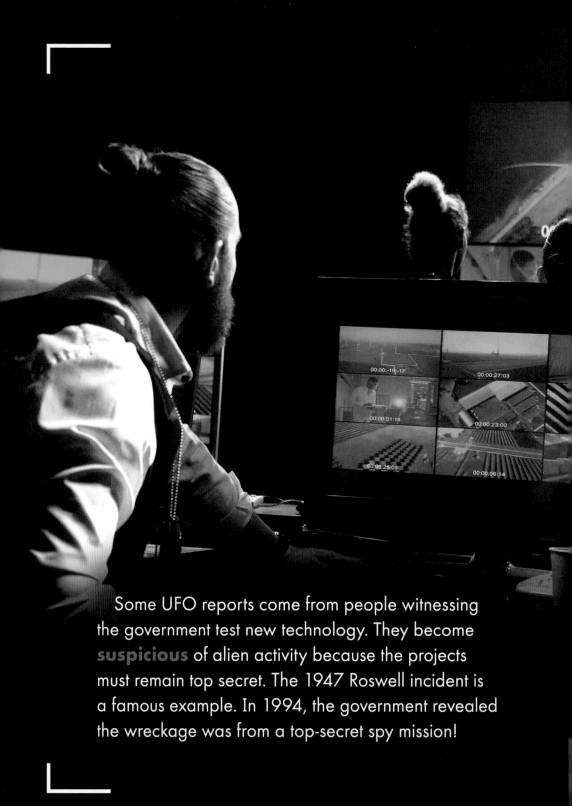

Some UFO reports come from people witnessing the government test new technology. They become **suspicious** of alien activity because the projects must remain top secret. The 1947 Roswell incident is a famous example. In 1994, the government revealed the wreckage was from a top-secret spy mission!

Some witnesses simply imagine seeing UFOs. In other cases, UFO sightings are faked. Photos do not always prove a sighting. Computer programs make it easy to change images to show things that did not happen.

fake UFO picture

UP IN THE AIR

A small number of credible cases remain unsolved. Their puzzling details and trustworthy witnesses leave investigators stumped. These cases are true UFOs. After all, the objects spotted are still unidentified. Whether or not they are alien is up for **debate**.

Ufologists worldwide have researched the phenomena for decades. Nobody has produced solid proof of alien visitors. But plenty are still trying. Research organizations are using new technology to study UFOs. Until they find new evidence, the existence of extraterrestrial UFOs remains up in the air.

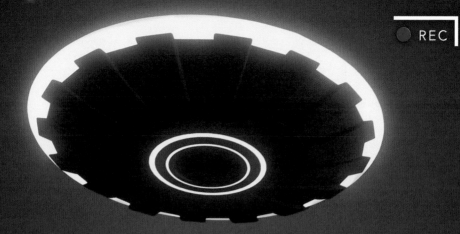

UFO CAPITAL OF THE WORLD

The government may have set the record straight about Roswell. Still, the city is known as the "UFO Capital of the World." It hosts a UFO Festival each summer!

GLOSSARY

aerial—appearing in the air

antenna—a device that sends or receives radio waves, often made of wire or metal

audio recorders—devices that capture and save sounds

credible—trustworthy

databases—online collections of information

debate—a discussion between people in which they share different opinions about something

evidence—information that helps prove or disprove something

extraterrestrial—coming from outside of Earth

investigation—the act of trying to find out the facts about something in order to learn if or how it happened

night-vision goggles—eyewear that magnifies light coming in to allow people to see in the dark

phenomena—unusual occurrences or events

physical—having an existence that can be seen, heard, smelled, tasted, or touched

polygraphs—devices used to test whether or not someone is telling the truth

radar—a device that uses radio waves to find and track objects

skeptics—people who doubt something is true

suspicious—having a feeling that something is wrong

telescope—a tube-shaped device used to see things that are far away, often in outer space

ufologists—people who study UFOs

wreckage—the broken or destroyed remains of an object

TO LEARN MORE

AT THE LIBRARY

Borgert-Spaniol, Megan. *UFOs: Are Alien Aircraft Overhead?*
Minneapolis, Minn.: Abdo Pub., 2018.

Kenney, Karen Latchana. *Mysterious UFOs and Aliens.*
Minneapolis, Minn.: Lerner Publications, 2018.

McCollum, Sean. *Handbook of UFOs, Crop Circles, and Alien
Encounters.* North Mankato, Minn.: Capstone Press, 2017.

ON THE WEB

Learning more about UFOs is as
easy as 1, 2, 3.

1. Go to www.factsurfer.com.

2. Enter "UFOs" into the search box.

3. Click the "Surf" button and you will see a list of
   related web sites.

With factsurfer.com, finding more information is just a click away.

INDEX

The images in this book are reproduced through the courtesy of: Fer Gregory, front cover; F.Schmidt, pp. 2-3; Iucentius, pp. 4-5; Ursatii, pp. 6 (UFO), 10-11, 28-29; FLUKY FLUKY, pp. 6-7 (people); leolintang, pp. 6-7; broukoid, p. 9 (UFO); Danieltaeger, pp. 10-11; Chronicle/ Alamy, pp. 11 (left), 13 (inset); Bettmann/ Getty, pp. 11 (right), 12-13, 15 (inset), 23 (inset); PunyaFamily, pp. 14-15; US government/ Wikipedia, p. 16 (inset); sripfoto, pp. 18-19; dani3315, pp. 20-21; Wavebreakmedia, p. 22 (woman); ultrapro/ Alamy, p. 22 (audio recorder); wdstock, pp. 22-23 (man); RobinsonBecquart, pp. 22-23; fabiodevilla, pp. 24-25; Thomas Barrat, p. 25 (left); Mette Fairgrieve, p. 25 (right); FrameStockFootages, pp. 26-27; Photo 12/ Alamy, p. 27.

Dodgeville Public Library
WITHDRAWN
Dodgeville, WI 53533